Ancient Roman Jobs

Brian Williams

Heinemann LIBRARY

www.heinemann.co.uk/library
Visit our website to find out more information about **Heinemann Library** books.

To order:
 Phone 44 (0) 1865 888066
Send a fax to 44 (0) 1865 314091
Visit the Heinemann Bookshop at www.heinemann.co.uk/library to browse our catalogue and order online.

First published in Great Britain by Heinemann Library, Halley Court, Jordan Hill, Oxford OX2 8EJ, part of Harcourt Education. Heinemann is a registered trademark of Harcourt Education Ltd.

Designed by Tinstar Design (www.tinstar.co.uk)
Illustrated by Jeff Edwards
Originated by Ambassador Litho Ltd
Printed by Wing King Tong in Hong Kong, China

ISBN 0 431 14563 6
06 05 04 03 02
10 9 8 7 6 5 4 3 2 1

British Library Cataloguing in Publication Data
Williams, Brian
    Ancient Roman jobs. – (People in the past)
    1. Occupations – Rome – History – Juvenile literature
    2. Civilization, Modern – Roman influences – Juvenile literature
    3. Rome – Social conditions – 510–30 B.C. – Juvenile literature
    I.Title
    331.7'00937

Acknowledgements
The Publishers would like to thank the following for permission to reproduce photographs:
AKG Photo, London pp17, 18, 22, 25, 30, 31, 32; Ancient Art & Architecture p8, 12, 20, 23, 27, 38, 41; Corbis p35; John Seely 26, 28, 39, 43; Scala Art Resource p6; Terry Griffiths & Magnet Harlequin pp14, 34, 36, 40; Trevor Clifford pp4, 7; Werner Foreman Archive / J Paul Getty Museum, Malibu p10.
Cover photograph reproduced with permission of AKG London.

Contents

Words appearing in the text in bold, **like this**, are explained in the Glossary.

An empire of farmers and builders

Who were the Romans? To us today, they are probably the most famous of all ancient peoples. The Romans believed their history began in 753 BC, that is 753 years before the birth of Jesus Christ. For almost 500 years they ruled one of the great **empires** of history.

The first Romans

The Romans lived in Italy. The first Romans were farmers, who lived in small villages on seven hills beside the River Tiber. These villages grew into a great city, Rome.

Rome became the centre of the world. It was a city of workers, and wherever they went, the Romans worked and built. They were great builders, and today across Europe, North Africa and the Middle East, the remains of Roman buildings can be seen. Others lie buried beneath fields or below the streets of modern cities.

From republic to empire

The first Romans were ruled by kings until 509 BC, when the people drove out their last king Tarquin the Proud. They set up a **republic**. Farmers and shepherds became **citizen**-soldiers of the republic. The Romans won wars against their neighbours, and conquered first all Italy, and then many other lands. From 27 BC, Rome was an empire, ruled by a leader with great power, the **emperor**.

The Romans built to last. The Colosseum, a huge **amphitheatre** in Rome, is still impressive 2000 years after it was built.

This map shows the Roman world in AD 100, when the empire was at its biggest. Most peoples in countries conquered by Rome copied Roman ways.

The Romans at work

Wealthy Romans had their housework done for them by servants called slaves. Slaves worked hard for no payment. Most Romans worked hard for an employer, such as a shopkeeper or farmer, or for themselves. They herded animals, grew crops, built homes and roads. They made all kinds of things – from swords for soldiers, to pots and knives for the kitchen.

In this book you will discover how Romans did these jobs, in a world with few machines. You will find out how Roman doctors and lawyers worked, and how people farmed, made bread and wine, and went fishing. You will explore Roman shops, and see how goods were made in workshops and factories. Prepare to be amazed by the feats of Roman construction engineering, and the way soldiers were trained. The Romans liked their fun too, and there were many entertainers, including the gladiators who fought and died for the amusement of the crowds in the arenas.

The Romans thought work was good for people. Men and women workers needed strong muscles, steady hands and keen eyes. Skills such as weaving, making clay pots, catching fish or baking bread were handed down from parents to children. Even people conquered by Rome admired the Romans' practical skills and the way they kept the peace. Yet the Romans thought of themselves as simple country people, like their farmer-ancestors. Rome's greatest lawyer, Cicero, said that farming was the best job for 'a free Roman'.

City workers

The city was the centre of Roman life, where trade was done and laws were made. The Romans built towns and cities in all the lands they ruled. The ruins of one small seaside town in Italy, Pompeii, are amazingly well preserved (see page 42). Here visitors can walk along streets and admire the town's neat, regular pattern. Most Roman towns were built on similar lines, with temples, baths, an **amphitheatre**, local government offices, and storehouses, as well as shops, workshops, inns and private houses.

Running the city

Slaves kept the cities clean. They swept the streets and collected waste from toilets in dung-carts – it was used along with animal dung to **manure** fields. Labourers dug ditches, repaired walls, and laid water pipes. Most towns had no public fire service, but the **Emperor** Augustus (who ruled from 27 BC to AD 14) started a fire brigade in Rome. He hired over 7000 men as policemen and firefighters.

City officials walked to work from their comfortable town houses, jostled in the narrow streets by poor workers hurrying from over-crowded apartments and rooms above shops. Politicians, lawyers, businessmen and **civil servants** headed for the Forum.

The Forum

This was the heart of the city. It was a large square, or open space where people could meet, talk politics, vote and do business. Workers were hired here, and every newcomer to town headed for the Forum to find out what was going on.

This carving from a Roman tomb shows people in serious conversation. Public speaking and debate played an important part in Roman life.

The Forum in Rome. This was the centre of government. Its great buildings included the Senate House, temples, basilicas and the Hall of Records. The open space in the centre was used as a market place.

The biggest building in the Forum was the temple-like **basilica**, which was both city hall and law court. This was the most important building in town, along with the main temple. Local workers' **guilds** also had their headquarters close to the centre of things. In Pompeii, the cloth-makers' building was second in size only to the basilica, showing how important cloth-making must have been to the town.

Relaxing after work

City officials were in charge of public services. Officials made sure the city's warehouses were full of basic foods such as flour, nuts, olive oil and wine. Others checked that the public baths were properly run. Many people went to the baths after the morning's work. They could bathe in hot and cold pools, have a massage, exercise in the *gymnasium*, and relax with friends. Slaves served drinks and snacks as the bathers 'unwound'.

Roman measures
Clerks checked weights and measures, to make sure shopkeepers and traders did not cheat customers. Romans measured length in units based on the human body – digit (finger-width), palm, foot, pace (two steps) and cubit (forearm). A Roman foot was 296 mm long. A thousand paces made one Roman mile (1480 metres). Weight was measured in *unciae* (ounces) and *librae* (pounds). A Roman *libra* (pound) equalled 327 grams.

Work on a villa

The Roman villa was a large house in the country, often with a farm attached. Seaside homes, like the grander houses in Pompeii, were also known as villas. Working farm-villas were Rome's food-factories.

How do we know?

There are ruined villas all over northern Europe. Here big-scale farming was more important than in the warmer Mediterranean region, where farms were mostly small. From finds made at **excavated** villa sites like Chedworth in England, and Settefinestre in Italy, we can picture what a villa-farm was like.

A working farm

A big villa was the centre of local life. The villa owner was a country gentleman, living with his family in 'the big house'. The farm was run by a manager, who had an office and lived with the farm workers in a separate part of the villa. Another part was set aside for storehouses and barns. These outbuildings included stores for hay, jars of oil and wine, sacks of grain, vegetables and fruit. There were sheds for farm animals too – cows, pigs, geese, chickens, sheep and goats.

Today, only ruins of this villa at Agrigento in Sicily can be seen. Two thousand years ago, this would have been a busy country farm-estate, producing food for the Roman **Empire**.

Rainy day jobs

The Roman writer Cato told villa owners how to keep workers busy. Even on wet days there would be plenty to do – storage jars need scrubbing out, floors swept, **manure** shovelled into neat heaps. Every so often, the owner should sell off old **oxen**, worn-out tools, and any slaves too old or too sick to work! 'A villa should always sell more than it buys' was Cato's advice.

The farm workers had to look after these animals through the farming year (shearing sheep, milking cows, feeding chickens and geese). They also worked in the fields – ploughing, sowing seed, harvesting, and tending vines and fruit trees. They were kept busy winter and summer, doing most of the work by hand.

Slaves belonged to the owner of the villa, who fed them but did not pay them. Some workers were free men and women, who worked for payment. They lived in small cottages, and also looked after small plots of land where they grew food for themselves.

The villa's produce

Villas produced food for the local district. In fields surrounding the villa, the workers grew crops of wheat and barley, used to make flour (for bread). There was often a fruit orchard with apple and pear trees and a vineyard with grapevines too. In the vegetable garden were rows of carrots, beans, onions and other vegetables.

Milk, meat and eggs from the farm were sold at the local market, and supplied to the soldiers at the nearest army **fort**. Every villa had a large granary (grain-store), where grain was stored to last through winter. Villa workers were among the most important in the local economy.

Slaves

Many people in the Roman world were not free to pick and choose a job. They were slaves, owned by masters and mistresses. Most Romans thought it was perfectly natural to keep slaves. How could their **empire** be run without slave labour?

Where slaves came from

Some people were born slaves, to slave mothers. Babies abandoned by their mothers were often raised as slaves. Other people were forced to become slaves. Rome's slave workers came from all over Europe, Africa and the Middle East. Many were kidnapped from their villages by pirates and slave-traders, who then sold them to slave owners. Prisoners of war, captured by the Roman army, were also put to work as slaves. After conquering Epirus in northern Greece in 167 BC, the Romans took over 150,000 Greek slaves to Rome.

Slaves were sold in slave markets to the highest bidder. A note hung around each slave's neck described any special skills the slave had. Educated slaves, skilled workers, or young men and girls sold for the highest prices.

A young slave holds a make-up box as she helps her mistress prepare to get ready. Many women worked as household slaves, often starting work as children.

The work of a slave

Slaves worked in homes, farms and workshops. Home slaves cleaned, cooked and served food, and washed clothes. They also did their mistress's hair, took messages, lit fires and looked after gardens. A wealthy Roman might keep up to 100 slaves in his town house, while some nobles owned as many as 10,000 slaves to work on their villas and country estates.

A few slaves lived fairly comfortable lives. An educated slave might work as tutor (teacher) to a rich family. Most slaves could not read or write, and did the dirtiest jobs. Slaves had no rights, and could be bought and sold, punished or even killed by their masters. The most wretched slaves worked in **quarries** and **mines**. Their work was hard, they were often badly treated and some were kept in chains to stop them running away.

Gaining freedom

Some Romans thought slavery was wrong. Many believed that a slave who was well fed and treated kindly would work better than a slave who was starved, dirty and beaten. Slaves who were well treated, and paid money by their owners, might save enough money to buy their freedom. Others were freed by their owners, as a thank you for their hard work. A man could go to a **magistrate** to arrange a slave's freedom, or he could free his slaves as part of his **will**.

Some more equal than others

A well-fed slave in the house of a kind family was better off than a starving free man. A few slaves became free men, went into business and ended up wealthy. However, most slaves were poor, and because they were not Roman **citizens**, had no rights in the eyes of the law. For hundreds of years, 'a slave was nothing'. Even after AD 212, when most conquered peoples were made citizens of Rome, slaves were still slaves – though new laws meant slaves were no longer treated cruelly.

Lawyers and politicians

The earliest known code, or set, of laws for Rome was drawn up in 450 BC. Roman schoolboys had to learn the most important ones by heart. Later Roman **emperors** changed old laws or made new ones, as they wished. There were so many laws that Roman lawyers were kept busy arguing over what the laws meant.

Roman laws were mostly based on common sense and local custom and on 'natural laws' which they thought were true for people everywhere. Roman ideas about the laws that govern us are still important today.

Governing Rome

The chief governing body of Rome was the **Senate**. At first senators were chosen by Rome's top leaders, the **Consuls**. Later, any man elected as a Quaestor (an official responsible for public finances) became a Senator. A Senator remained a Senator for life, unless found guilty of a crime.

Another assembly called the *Comitia Tributa* represented noblemen and ordinary **citizens**. It elected government officials, including Consuls (who led the army), Aediles (in charge of public works), and Tribunes (who looked after the ordinary people's interests).

The remains of the forum at Trieste in Italy. In roman towns, the forum complex often included a large building called a *basilica*. These were used as markets, courthouses and meeting places.

The lawyer Marcus Tullius Cicero was admired for the brilliance of his speeches, and for his elegant writing in Latin. He made his name in 70 BC by prosecuting the dishonest governor of Sicily. Cicero became Consul in 63 BC, but his criticism annoyed the ruling aristocrats, who banished him for a year. When he continued to speak out against their bad rule, Rome's rulers had him murdered.

Roman towns had their own local governments, and politicians seeking election campaigned by making speeches in the Forum or on street corners. From graffiti found in the ruins of Roman towns such as Pompeii, we know that politicians' supporters scrawled messages on walls such as 'vote for Claudius'!

Roman emperors reduced the power of the Senate, and chose their own friends as Senators – by the AD 300s there were about 2000 Senators, including men from Spain, Gaul, Roman Asia and Roman Africa. Many of the most important Senators were landowners, who seldom bothered to travel to Rome for Senate meetings. In the end, the Senate became little more than Rome's city council. Thousands of **civil servants** worked to keep the **empire** running from day to day.

Scramble for the top

Politics in Rome was for rich men (women did not take a public part). Some ambitious politicians spent fortunes on public entertainment, such as gladiator fights, to win votes and the cheers of the crowds. **Bribery** of officials and electors was common. Often an unscrupulous politician would rake up (or invent) a scandal to disgrace a rival. Murdering a political opponent was not uncommon!

Lawyers in court

Criminals stood trial before an elected judge called a **magistrate**. So-called crimes against the state, such as treason (plotting to kill the emperor or aid an enemy country) or stealing money from the government, were heard by a commission of enquiry. Lawyers studied at law school. Rome had the world's first fee-paid professional lawyers, and a clever lawyer could become very rich. If he won a treason trial, he was rewarded with a fourth of the loser's property. However, if he upset powerful rulers like Cicero did, he could end up dead!

Doctors

A Roman doctor relied on a mixture of common sense, superstition and doing what had worked before. Doctors did not understand the causes of disease. If a medicine worked last time, and the patient got better, then they would try the same treatment again. All Roman doctors were men, though there were women midwives, who helped mothers give birth to their babies.

Useful and useless medicines

Some medicines were based on plants. Poppy seed juice was given to crying babies (it sent them to sleep). The modern pain-killing drug morphine is made from poppy seeds. Willow bark was used to lower a fever (it contained aspirin).

Other medicines were quite useless. Fat from dead cats and snakes were sold as a cure for baldness. The worse the medicine smelled, or the more expensive, the better it was thought to be.

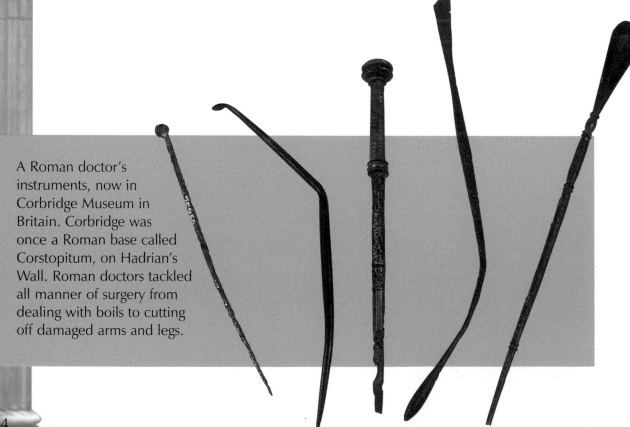

A Roman doctor's instruments, now in Corbridge Museum in Britain. Corbridge was once a Roman base called Corstopitum, on Hadrian's Wall. Roman doctors tackled all manner of surgery from dealing with boils to cutting off damaged arms and legs.

Rome's greatest doctor

Rome's most famous doctor was Galen. He began to study medicine when he was 16. He learned much about surgery while treating the wounds of gladiators. He was one of the first doctors to study **anatomy**, by cutting up the bodies of dead animals. Doctors were not allowed to cut up human bodies. Galen wrote over 100 medical books, and medical students used his book on anatomy until the 1500s. At the age of 31, Galen went to live in Rome, where he gave lectures on medicine and became personal doctor to the **emperors** Marcus Aurelius and Commodus.

Public Health

The Romans blamed bad health on bad air, bad smells, bad water, dirty bodies and damp ground. They drained marshes, which was a good idea, even though they did not realise that it was mosquitoes, not marshes, that caused malaria fever in people. They did their best to keep towns free from rubbish. They built **aqueducts** to bring fresh water into towns, and filtered drinking water if it had to be drawn from muddy streams.

Who were Rome's doctors?

Tombstones reveal who some of Rome's doctors were. Many were Greeks, and many had been slaves before gaining their freedom. Some were still slaves. The fact that so many doctors were Greek alarmed some Romans, who refused to be treated by a Greek in case the doctor tried to poison them! After Julius Caesar allowed Greek doctors to become Roman **citizens** in 46 BC, people thought more highly of them.

Hospitals

There were hospitals for soldiers in army **forts**, and some of the best doctors in the Roman world were army surgeons. They used surgical instruments similar to some still used in operations today. There were fewer hospitals for civilians. People seeking a cure would spend the night in a temple dedicated to the god of healing, Asclepius. Prayer and gifts to the god, they thought, would be just as useful as a doctor's medicine.

Writers and historians

Educated Romans wrote letters to friends and relatives, though most ordinary people never learned to read and write. For short letters, people wrote on tablets of soft wax with a pointed stick or stylus. A two-sided writing tablet was hinged to open like a book. A person wrote a message on one side, sent it, and received an answer written on the other side.

For long letters, Romans wrote with pen and ink. The ink was made from soot, gum and water. The pen or stylus was made from a sharpened reed or goose's feather. For writing paper, the Romans used sheets of **papyrus**.

The mail
Important people **dictated** official letters to a secretary. There was a messenger service for government letters, while an ordinary **citizen** would send a slave to deliver a letter, or give the letter to a friend travelling in the right direction. It took about thirty-three days for a letter from Britain to get to Rome.

Poet of Rome
Virgil was Rome's most famous poet. His full name was Publius Vergilius Maro. He had trained to be a lawyer, but was too shy to stand up in court, and so became a poet instead. Poems earned less money than lawsuits, but luckily Virgil was befriended by a rich nobleman, who gave him a house and money. Virgil wrote a long poem *The Aeneid*, an epic about the Trojan hero Aeneas and the founding of Rome. He also wrote poems called *The Georgics*, about country life, which are full of facts on such matters as how to keep bees and how to make grape vines grow well.

Professional writers

Much of what we know about Rome comes from the writings of professional writers, who included poets, scientists and **historians**. Like writers today, most expected to be paid. One street in Rome, the Argiletum, was famous for its bookshops. Booksellers pasted adverts for new books on walls and pillars. There were also publishers, like Titus Pomponius Atticus who published books by Cicero, and they made sure no one copied their authors' books without payment.

Every copy of a book had to be copied by hand, because the Romans had no printing machines. A slave copied the words onto sheets of papyrus or **parchment**. Each finished sheet was glued to the one before, so that the book ended up as a long roll, or scroll. It was wound onto two wooden rods, and unrolled to read. Unsold books ended up as wrapping paper!

Famous writers

Writers in Rome relied on help from rich friends, unless they were rich themselves. Catullus was one of Rome's most successful poets. He owned two big houses and a pleasure boat, but complained that he was always short of money! The Romans liked to be told about the great events and people of their history. They enjoyed reading the history books of Livy and Tacitus, and the poetry of Virgil.

This wall painting from Pompeii shows a Roman couple, the man holding a scroll book or *volumen*, the woman with a hinged wax writing tablet (for letters). They are believed to be a lawyer and his wife.

Priests and priestesses

The Romans took religion seriously, at home and in public. They believed in household spirits, who protected the home, and in great gods like the sky god Jupiter and Mars, god of war. Many of these gods were borrowed from the Greeks (Jupiter was the Greek god Zeus, for example). For a time, the **emperor** himself was treated as a god. By the AD 300s, many people in the Roman **Empire** had turned to Christianity.

Roman priests

Before Romans became Christians, the job of the priest or *pontifex* was to look after the temple of a god, and make **sacrifices**. To make a sacrifice, the priest killed a bull, a sheep or a pig, as an offering to the god. The priest also carried out special ceremonies inside the temple, such as burning sweet-smelling incense, saying prayers, and making gifts of flowers and food brought by worshippers to the god's statue.

Priests in Rome belonged to groups called colleges. The top college was headed by the high priest, or *Pontifex Maximus*. This post was often given to an important politician, such as Julius Caesar, who was chosen as Pontifex Maximus in 63 BC. The work of the college of priests included publishing a yearly calendar of events, including important religious festivals and holidays.

This wall carving shows a Roman priest (right) at the altar-table, preparing a sacrifice to a god.

Watching what you ate

Each important god or goddess had a special priest, called a *flamen*. A flamen had to obey many rules. The priest of Jupiter (king of the gods) was not allowed to go outdoors bareheaded. He could never touch, or even mention by name, raw meat, ivy, a female goat or beans! A priest had to be especially careful when performing a ceremony, such as the sacrifice of an animal, because if he did it wrongly, the god would be displeased.

Looking for omens

Priests known as *augurs* claimed to be able to look into the future. Their job was to discover how the gods felt about Rome. They looked for magical signs in the flight of birds, the colour of the sun, or the insides of animals killed as sacrifices. They interpreted these as **omens,** sent by the gods, which could be read as 'good news' or 'bad news'. Most Romans believed in **astrology**. They would pay an astrologer to read their 'star-signs' before planning a journey or simply to see what tomorrow would bring.

The Vestals

Most priests were men. However, a girl from a respectable family might be chosen to be a Vestal priestess. There were six Vestals, who watched over the sacred fire in the Temple of Vesta, goddess of the hearth. Keeping the 'home fire burning' was very important to Romans as a symbol of family life and civilization. Every family worshipped Vesta at home.

Temple of the sacred fire

The shrine to Vesta was one of Rome's most sacred places. It was in the Forum in Rome, and only women could enter its innermost room. In this temple, a sacred fire was kept burning day and night and watched over by the Vestal priestesses. The Vestals also fetched water from a sacred spring and looked after the shrine. A girl was chosen to become a Vestal when she was between 6 and 10 years old, and she usually remained a Vestal priestess for 30 years. She was forbidden to marry. If she did, she was buried alive. Even after a Vestal 'retired', it was thought unlucky for her to marry.

The farmer

The Romans started off as farmers and shepherds, and never lost their love of the 'simple' country life. Writers such as the poet Virgil and Lucius Columella wrote about the farmer's tasks. These writers, and pictures on walls and monuments, tell us a lot about Roman farming.

Roman farming

In spring, farmers prepared fields in strips, using heavy ploughs pulled by **oxen**. They sowed seed by hand. Farm tools included iron spades and hoes, wooden rakes and, for cutting grass and wheat, **sickles** and two-handed **scythes**. Roman farmers invented a 'wheat-cutting' machine, called the *vallus*. The *vallus* was a two-wheeled cart, pushed from behind by a horse or mule. At the front of the cart was a saw-toothed cutting blade. One worker walked behind to steer, while another in front collected the cut stalks as they fell into the machine's 'grass box'.

Crops and cattle

The Romans took crops from Asia and the Mediterranean all over Europe. Roman-British farmers grew cabbages, parsnips, and carrots – foods new to Britain.

Ceres was the Roman goddess who taught people to plough, sow, reap, and bake bread. She was usually shown carrying a sheaf of corn (as in this statue), a symbol of fruitfulness.

Roman farmers also bred bigger cattle and sheep, which provided more meat, milk and skins. Italy's Chianina cattle, a giant breed still kept today, are probably related to the strong oxen used by Roman farmers to pull ploughs and loads. From finds of animal bones on Roman farm sites, it seems that oxen were four times as numerous as horses. Horses were too expensive for most farmers.

The Romans practised a simple **crop rotation**. If they grew wheat in a field one year, they planted lupins, peas or beans the next then returned to wheat in the third year. This system helped keep the soil fertile.

Farm work

Most farm work was done by hand. Harvest time was hard work for everyone. Workers threshed the wheat with **flails**, (to separate the tasty grain from the outer skin or **chaff**). They tossed the grain into the air (this is called 'winnowing'), to let the wind blow away more dust and chaff.

Some of this work was done by machine. One threshing machine, pulled by oxen, had a heavy frame with nails sticking out underneath. Another had a toothed roller, which crunched over the grain.

Lucius Columella, the farm book author

Columella tells us a lot about Roman farming. He lived in the first century AD. Born in Spain, he took up farming in Italy, after serving in the Roman army as a soldier. Columella wrote more than 12 books about farming, describing the best ways to plant crops, keep fish and bees, and make wine and cheese.

Makers of food

A good harvest meant plenty of food. A bad harvest could mean people went hungry. As Roman cities grew bigger, more people bought their food, instead of growing it themselves. Food trades, such as baking and winemaking, employed people in every Roman town. Basic foods – bread, olive oil and wine – were produced in enormous quantities.

The baker

Grain from cereal crops, such as wheat or rye, was made into flour to make bread. The Romans ate a lot of bread. Many people made bread at home, but there were also bakers in every town. Large bakers' ovens, made from brick, tiles and clay, and heated by fires of logwood and charcoal, have been found in London, Pompeii and many other Roman towns.

People also bought flour from the local miller and baked bread in ovens at home. The Roman oven was beehive-shaped, and was heated by burning wood or charcoal inside. When the oven was really hot, the ashes were raked out, and the bread and pies were put in. The oven door was closed and the baking was left to cook as the oven slowly cooled.

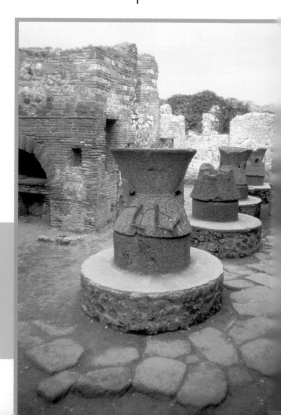

From millstones found at Pompeii, we know that it was common for families to grind their own flour, using grindstones. So they were always sure of having flour for baking.

The bakery of Modestus, at Pompeii. The spool-shaped objects are stone mills for grinding grain. The top stone was turned by slaves or a donkey, to crush the grain into flour. The flour was then mixed with water to make dough, and baked into round, flat loaves of bread in the baker's oven.

Sunny hillsides were used for vinegrowing, and the lava from volcanoes provided rich soil for grapes. This mosaic from Pompeii shows slaves treading grapes to make wine, a September task.

Wine makers

Grapes and olives were the most important fruits in the Roman world. The Romans grew grapes to eat and to make wine. They planted grapes wherever it was warm and sunny, along the rivers Rhine and Danube, and as far north as Britain. The grapes were picked by hand, and for winemaking were then pressed to squeeze out the juice. This was done by slaves treading them in a big tub (a method still used into modern times), and by heavy screw-presses. The wine was left to ferment and then put into wooden barrels, pottery jars or goatskins. Romans did not keep wine in bottles (glass was too precious). They usually drank wine the year it was made. Roman wine did not taste good if older than a year or two.

Olive oil had many uses

Olive trees grow best in warm lands, and farmers grew olives all over the Mediterranean world. The Romans liked to eat olives, but also crushed the fruit in a screw press, to squeeze out the oil. Olive oil was used in Roman cooking (just as it is in cooking today). It was even more important as a fuel for burning in oil lamps. Bathers rubbed olive oil into their skins, and then scraped off the mixture of oil and dirt (the Romans did not have soap).

Fishermen and sailors

The Romans' 'home sea' was the Mediterranean Sea, rich in fish and seafood. Sea animals are often shown on wall paintings and **mosaic** floor decorations. Fishermen went out in small boats, to catch fish, octopus, crabs, lobsters and other sea animals. Sailors in sailing ships criss-crossed the Mediterranean between Italy and Africa, and travelled along the coasts of other lands.

A taste for seafood

Seafood was a favourite meal in Roman times. There were seafood shops like the one discovered at the Roman town of Wroxeter in England. Romans went out with three-pronged spears to catch eels in rivers, and set basket traps and nets. Full-time fishermen went fishing for a living, often fishing at night and bringing the fish each morning to sell in the town market. A seaside town like Pompeii always had fresh fish for sale, and oysters too, raised in oyster 'farms' in the Bay of Naples. Rich Romans had their own fish ponds, where fish were raised and fattened, so they could eat fresh fish whenever they felt like it. In summer, fish quickly went bad, so it was often dried or salted to preserve it.

Going to sea

Some Romans went to work at sea, as sailors. Ships could always be seen sailing along the coasts. Many towns in the Roman world, like Pompeii, depended on sea trade. Roman London grew rapidly as a river port after AD 60, and **archaeologists** have been able to reconstruct what the waterfront, with its **quays** and storehouses, looked like. A port like this provided work for many people, loading and unloading ships, and repairing them.

The sailors' god

Romans believed the sea god Neptune lived in a palace beneath the waves. With his trident (a three-pronged spear), he could raise storms. Sailors prayed to Neptune to keep them safe. **Altars** bearing his symbols of a dolphin and trident were sunk at the mouths of harbours and rivers to bring good luck to ships.

Roman sailors learned how to work the sails and oars, find their way using the stars and landmarks, and be ready to fight off pirates! The sea was full of dangers. A sailor feared storms, sea monsters and evil spirits, like the **sirens** who sang to bewitch passing mariners. No wonder sailors prayed to the sea god Neptune, and carried lucky charms!

What kind of boats did Romans sail?

Buried in River Thames mud in London, archaeologists have found remains of Roman ships. One was a sailing barge used to carry building stone. A coin dated AD 88–89 had been put beneath the mast by the builders, for luck. Boat builders went on doing this right up to modern times.

From pictures and archaeological finds, we know that Roman merchant ships were broad and fat, with a single sail, and a stern post that curved upwards, like a swan's neck. Some were very big. A ship shown on a tombstone at Pompeii must have been over 50 metres long.

Tomb paintings show boats used by their owners. This painting from the tomb of a ferryman named Arascanius shows the kind of boat the Romans used to cross rivers and to unload cargo from big merchant ships. On the left, slaves are carrying goods onto Arascanius's boat.

Shopkeepers

For the Romans, daily shopping was a chance to meet friends and gossip. The main streets of a Roman town were lined with shops, bars, restaurants and workshops. Many were family businesses. The family owned its shop, and often lived in rooms behind or above the business. A sign hung over the entrance showed people what the shop sold: for example, a sandal for a shoemaker, a bunch of grapes for a wine-seller.

The shops in town

Roman shops had open fronts. They had counters for displaying the goods on sale, and stone benches or wooden stools for customers to sit on. Romans went shopping for fresh food, such as bread, meat, fish, and vegetables. A shopper might also want to buy household items, such as spoons and knives, cloth, and olive oil for lamps. Stalls selling takeaway hot meals were popular, since many poor people had no means of cooking at home. At Pompeii, sauce jars have been found with inscriptions telling customers the jars contained 'Quality Strained Sauce'.

Bars and taverns

Bars sold drinks, and taverns (inns) offered food and a bed for the night. 'Asellina's Bar' in Pompeii (the name Asellina was scratched on the plaster wall) still has its stone counter, with holes to hold the large pottery jars, called *amphorae*, in which the wine was kept.

In Pompeii, shoppers used large stepping stones to cross the street when the road was wet. The roads could be filled up by heavy rain, but also served as drains to carry away much of the town's rubbish. The stones were spaced so cartwheels would pass between them.

This picture, cut in stone, shows a Roman butcher's shop. The butcher is chopping up meat on a three-legged wooden block (a kind still used today by some butchers). Behind him are his balance scales, for weighing the meat.

Hurrah for profit

A middle-sized town the size of Pompeii (population: approximately 20,000) had flour-millers, bakers, fruit and vegetable shops, butchers, and sellers of game (wild animals such as pigeons, ducks and hares). There were clothes shops and jewellers, and also men's hairdressers. Women normally had their hair done at home.

Pompeii also had leather-workers, perfume-sellers, plumbers, decorators, and at least one surgeon. Shopkeepers scrawled on walls to advertise anything specially good or cheap. Business was the key to success. On a wall in Pompeii, someone wrote 'Hurrah for profit'.

Making money

Roman shoppers used money – gold, silver, brass and copper coins made in mints run by the government. From 27 BC, Roman coins were stamped with the head of the **emperor**. The Romans did not use banks like we have today, but there were moneylenders who would lend money, but charged **interest**.

The busy workshops

A Roman city was noisy from dawn to dusk. Bakers were among the first people to start work, baking bread. All day long, street traders shouted out prices to attract customers. Carts rumbled over the stony streets, metalworkers hammered, builders banged and carpenters sawed.

Trades and traders

The Romans made most of the things they needed in small workshops. If a woman wanted new shoes, she went to the shoemaker. The shoemaker might have sandals or boots in her size, or he might make her a pair, using leather he had bought from the tanner.

Inside the *fullonica*, or cloth-workshop, owned by Stephanus of Pompeii. The large stone bath was used for soaking and washing new cloth. The cloth was treated with a mixture of soda and human urine – there was a jar outside the shop for men to use, to make sure of a free supply of urine.

In the same way, if a cook wanted a new dish, he could choose from the potter's display or ask for a dish to be made specially. The potter worked in wet clay, shaping the dish by hand. To harden the dish, he 'fired' it inside a hot oven. The most famous Roman pottery, a red-glazed kind called Samian ware, was first made at Arretium (Arezzo) in Italy. It was so popular that special factories were set up to make it.

Busy, busy workers

Almost every Roman town had workshops. Inside, workers were busy making everyday items such as candles, lamps, wooden furniture and clothing. There were small factories making pots, rugs and tapestries, though most women did their own **spinning** and weaving at home. Factories called armouries made weapons and armour for soldiers. In many towns, there were public laundries, where workers washed and pressed clothes.

Pompeii's cloth trade

Pompeii had a busy cloth industry, with several workshops for the dyeing and preparation of cloth. These workshops were called *fullonicae*, and one of the best-preserved workshops in Pompeii is the Fullonica Stephani, which belonged to a 'fuller' named Stephanus. It was like a laundry, with large water tanks for washing the cloth to get rid of grease. One of the ingredients in the washing was **urine**, collected and brought to the fuller's shop in jars. Clothmaking was a long and messy process, almost as smelly as making leather (tanning).

Smelly trades

Pompeii had a fish-sauce factory, where workers made *garum*, the fish sauce Romans liked on their food. It must have been one of the smelliest buildings in town. Even smellier were the tanners. Tanners (leather-makers) had to work outside town, because of the awful smell from the tanks in which they softened the skins of cattle, sheep and goats.

Miners and metalworkers

To build a temple or a palace required hundreds of cartloads of sand, cement, and stone. To make tools and weapons, the Romans needed metals such as lead, tin, copper, zinc and iron. All these materials had to be dug from underground, in **mines** and **quarries**, along with silver and gold, and (cheaper but just as vital) salt.

Slaves and prisoners toiled in quarries, cutting stones, and in the mines. Some miners worked bent double in tunnels lit only by flickering oil lamps. With no explosives, they relied on picks and hammers to smash the rock. Or they might light a fire, heating the rock, then throw water or vinegar over it. Sudden cooling would split the rock. Many miners were killed in accidents, by falling rocks. Others simply dropped from exhaustion. They were beaten by cruel **overseers** if they stopped work and were given little food. Being sent to the mines was often a sentence of death.

Working in a gold mine

From **archaeologists'** discoveries, we know a lot about one gold mine in Roman Britain, at Dolaucothi in Wales. Here miners dug tunnels 40 metres underground, using hand-pumps to stop the water flooding the tunnels. The water flowed to the mine along three **aqueducts** (one 11 kilometres long). In workshops close to the mine, jewellers and goldsmiths turned some of the gold into armbands, necklaces and rings. The rest of the gold went to the mint, to be made into coins.

This tombstone in York shows a blacksmith working at his forge. He would hammer the hot metal on an anvil to beat into the shape he wanted.

A bronze statue shows Romulus and Remus, legendary founders of Rome, who were raised as babies by a wolf. Melted bronze was poured into moulds to make statues like this.

The smith at work

Iron was the most useful metal to the Romans, though they also used a lot of bronze and probably knew how to make steel as well. The iron was smelted (melted out of its rocky ore) in a furnace. The iron-maker used foot-worked **bellows** to puff air into the fire to make it hotter. He ended up with a lump of soft iron, which he hammered into shape to make a bar of wrought iron.

A metalworker, or smith, worked in a forge. It was hot, smoky and steamy. The smith went on hammering, cooling and reheating the metal until he was satisfied with the shape and hardness of the sword or axe he was making. There was a blacksmith (metalworker) in almost every Roman town.

Higher-paid workers made ornamental metalwork for rich Romans, including expensive decorated armour, for generals to wear at parades, and elegant jewellery. Romans made wire, not as we do today by drawing the metal through holes, but by beating it into paper-thin plates and cutting it into thin strips.

The blacksmith god

Because it involved fire and smoke (and often went wrong), metalworking was regarded as a mysterious craft – rather like magic. Metalworkers had a favourite god. He was Vulcan, Roman god of fire, who made the gods' armour and swords using magical powers. Vulcan could start fires too – like a careless blacksmith!

Moving about

The Romans are famous for their excellent roads. The army was in charge of road building. Army roads were built so that soldiers could march quickly to any troublespot in the **empire**, but any traveller could use them. The army engineers made sure the roads were well maintained. Tunnels and bridges were repaired, and roadside trees cut back, so no robbers could lie in wait for travellers.

Wagon drivers

The 'truck driver' of the Roman world drove a heavy wooden wagon pulled by **oxen**, or a smaller cart. A farmer going into market would drive his own cart, full of fruit and vegetables. It had two solid wooden wheels and was pulled by a pair of oxen or mules. For heavy goods, such as a load of building stone or a delivery of wine-skins, a driver would be sent out by his employer in a creaking and slow-moving *serracum*, a four-wheeled cart pulled by a team of as many as eight oxen. The army had its own wagon-units to carry military stores between forts, while army officers dashed around in two-wheeled chariots, throwing up clouds of dust in summer.

A Roman wagon-driver with his wagon and oxen. Oxen were very strong but plodded along rather slowly. They were harnessed to the wagon by a shoulder harness called a yoke. Often the driver would walk alongside or in front of his oxen.

The innkeeper

A road journey took days or even weeks. So where did travellers spend the night? There were inns along main roads. Some innkeepers kept clean, comfortable lodgings. However, most inns were dirty and rowdy. People complained of drunken fellow travellers, and were frightened to stay at an inn for fear of thieves making off with their valuables. Rich people preferred to sleep in a friend's house.

Getting around

Donkey-drivers walked with their donkeys, each animal carrying a pack on its back. On the road they would meet many travellers on foot, some pushing handcarts or carrying baskets and bundles, and a few richer people riding their own horses. A family moving house would hire a covered wagon called a *raeda*. Inside, the passengers were shaded from the sun and rain, but it was a slow, bumpy journey. In big cities, there was a kind of taxi service. A rich person not wanting to walk might hire a *cisium*, a fast two-wheeled chariot pulled by two horses. A wealthy lady might choose to be carried in a **litter** by eight slaves.

Water travel

Boatmen moved heavy loads, such as stone and timber, by boat. This was the cheapest way to move heavy goods. Sail-barges were used on rivers. In places where there was no bridge, ferrymen carried passengers from one side of a river to the other.

Roman merchant ships were slow and a sailor was away from home for weeks at a time. A voyage from Ostia in Italy across the Mediterranean Sea to Carthage in Africa took about three days. A ship's captain would take paying passengers too, though most travellers (being scared of drowning) usually went as far as they could by road.

Engineers and builders

The Romans were superb builders. They made the best roads in the ancient world, and amazingly long and high **aqueducts** – arched bridges for carrying water into a town. They built towns, harbours, palaces, temples, public baths, fortresses, and **amphitheatres**.

Building in stone and concrete

Workers cut stone into blocks, which they then set into mortar, a mixture of sand and lime. During the 3rd century BC, Roman engineers discovered how to make cement that would set hard even under water. This was very useful for building harbours. Roman builders mixed crushed stone with cement to make concrete, and used it as a cheaper alternative to stone.

Brick and tile makers

Bricks and tiles were made from clay baked in ovens called kilns, or dried in the hot sun. Unlike a shoemaker (who could work alone, perhaps with one or two apprentices), a tile-maker ran a small factory with a team of workers. Some men dug the clay. Others built and heated the kilns. The most skilled workers shaped the tiles in moulds, and 'fired' them in the kilns. Yet more workers stacked the finished tiles, and delivered them to their buyer.

The most common tiles were roof tiles, and the special tiles used in Roman central heating systems. Roman bricks and tiles were so well made that some Roman brickwork is still standing, and Roman tiles are often found reused in much later buildings. Walls and floors were decorated with patterns of **mosaics**.

Building tools found at Hadrian's Wall in Britain. Roman building workers used chisels (centre), hammers, hand drills, iron nails (left) and wooden pegs. Also pictured is a a trowel and a hammerhead.

Roman cranes

Roman builders had few machines. They did use wooden cranes to hoist stones and heavy timber. The crane had a long lifting arm, with a rope wound around a drum at the centre of a large wooden wheel. The wheel was turned by men walking inside it. As the wheel turned, the rope was wound around the drum, and lifted the load. Builders also erected scaffolding and used ropes and pulleys to lift heavy stones into position.

Roman roads

Roman roads were built by the army for the army. **Surveyors** mapped the path of a new road, and they liked to choose as straight a line as possible. Their instruments included a portable sundial (for telling the time by the sun) and a *groma*, an instrument with weighted 'plumb lines' used to check that the line of the road was straight. Soldiers usually dug out the roadbed and then laid sand and stones for the foundations, finally laying paving stones on top. The road surface was cambered (sloped) so rainwater drained off into a ditch at the side. Some Roman roads were still in use a thousand years after they were built!

The Pantheon in Rome had a concrete dome 43 metres across – the largest in the world for almost 1800 years. Exactly how it was built remains the builders' secret. The Pantheon was a temple and is now a church.

The soldier

Many Romans made a career in the Roman army. So did many non-Romans, who were recruited to help defend the **Empire**. A soldier's weapons, clothes, and food were supplied, though the cost came out of his pay. There was not a lot of money left over for luxuries.

The legionary

Soldiers of the elite Roman **legions** were called legionaries. A legionary had to be a Roman **citizen**. A legionary was not supposed to marry, but most did. If a soldier was sent to a foreign land, his wife and children had to manage as best they could. Many soldiers serving on the frontiers set up home with local women, although in theory this was against the law.

Each legion was commanded by a **legate**, a senior officer who was often the governor of a **province**. Junior officers were called tribunes. The legion had its office staff of clerks and a medical unit. The men who really ran the army were the **centurions**, each of whom commanded a 'century' of 80 to 100 men.

An altar to the Roman war god Mars, found at Housesteads on Hadrian's Wall in Britain. Roman soldiers prayed to Mars to bring them victory in battle. They would have made offerings at this altar to please Mars.

A hard life

Even after leaving the army, an old soldier might still be 'called up' if there was war. Retired soldiers complained that the 'farmland' they were given would not grow anything. German soldiers demanding higher pay in AD 15 said 'war is dreadful and peace is a bore without profit' – meaning they were better off fighting, when they at least had the chance of some loot!

The auxiliary

An **auxiliary** was a soldier who was not a Roman citizen, though he could become one after 25 years' service. He was paid only a third as much as a legionary, and was not so well trained. Many auxiliaries guarded frontier posts. Others were 'specialists' with weapons such as bows and arrows, or slingshots.

What soldiers did

The Roman soldier was trained to fight. Discipline was strict. The legionary learned to march, ride a horse, and build a camp. He also learned many useful skills, and became as good at building bridges or roads as he was at fighting with sword and spear.

In camp, Roman soldiers lived in **barracks**, just like many soldiers today. Eight men lived together in a barrack room, and also shared a mule, to carry their tent and a millstone for grinding corn. All soldiers had to do routine jobs such as cleaning toilets and tidying up the barracks – unless he was a blacksmith or an arrow-maker. A legionary's weapons, clothes and food were provided, but he had to pay for them out of his salary – which included an allowance of salt (Latin *salarium* – which is how we get the word salary). If he survived, after 25 years he could retire, often to a 'colony' of old soldiers, and become a farmer.

Roman entertainers

Roman entertainment included some shows people would not find entertaining today. Roman **emperors** spent fortunes on 'spectacles' held in vast arenas, like the Colosseum in Rome, to keep the people amused. Armies of workers, mostly slaves, worked 'backstage' to organize these shows. Some spectacles involved flooding the arena to stage mock sea-battles between real ships manned by criminals (who were freed if they fought well). The arena workers also had to look after wild animals, such as lions, bears, rhinoceroses and elephants. The animals were made to fight one another or matched against gladiators.

Street entertainers

There were less bloodthirsty entertainments. In towns, innkeepers provided drink, music and gambling games for travellers, and for townsfolk looking for company and relaxation. Street musicians, acrobats and jugglers entertained in the marketplace. For a dinner party, a wealthy Roman could hire clowns, musicians and dancers to amuse his guests while they dined. These entertainers were both men and women.

A **mosaic** from a house in Pompeii shows Roman actors rehearsing a play. Two men on the left are practising dance steps. A musician plays the double pipes, and on the right an actor is being dressed in his costume. The man sitting down has two masks beside him. Could he perhaps be the author?

Chariot racing

One of the most dangerous Roman jobs was chariot racing, a sport popular all over the Roman **Empire**. In Rome over 250,000 people packed the Circus Maximus to watch the thrilling races. Many drivers were injured or killed in smashes as the chariots hurtled around the seven laps of the 550-metre oval track. Fans cheered on their favourite. A winning (and lucky) charioteer became a rich sporting superstar. An inscription written to honour a famous Spanish charioteer, Gaius Apulleius Diocles, tells us that in 24 years he won over 1000 of his 4000 races.

Actors and the theatre

The theatre was popular and noisy – Roman audiences liked rather crude plays and lots of action. During one play over 600 mules paraded across the stage! They preferred **comedies** to **tragedies**. In a Roman theatre, plays were performed in daytime, usually on festival days, when shops were closed. The theatre was free (it was government-funded), but the best seats were kept for **senators** and nobles.

Many actors were slaves, recruited by the theatre managers, and their status was lowly. Most Romans did not think acting a respectable job, even for a male slave! The most famous Roman actor was a man named Roscius, who died in 62 BC. His style was to 'over-act' wildly, and this was true of most Roman actors. They wore masks to help the audience tell the difference between good and bad characters. Costumes also 'fixed' a character. An old man wore white, a young man purple, a female character yellow. So did the actors' wigs – white for old men, black for young men, red for slaves. To sit through a play lasting several hours, Romans brought soft cushions and picnics, and might chatter so much that the actors had to shout to make themselves heard.

Women were allowed to act in short plays called mimes, in which they sang and danced. In a Roman pantomime, singers told a familiar **myth** through song and dance, while one actor did all the actions, never saying a word.

Gladiators

Gladiator-fights began in Rome in 264 BC, and became hugely popular during the later **Empire**. **Emperors** put on expensive and bloody 'amusements' to keep the people happy.

Life of a gladiator

Gladiators were trained to fight in the arena. The arena (*harena* in Latin) was actually the middle part of the **amphitheatre**, or stadium. It was covered with sand, so that the gladiators would not slip. Most gladiators were criminals, prisoners of war or slaves. A few were free men who chose to become gladiators. Some became as popular as today's sports stars, and the most successful fighters were allowed to retire, with the gift of a wooden sword. For most gladiators, however, death in the arena ended their careers.

Gladiators were trained in special gladiator schools. From a gladiator school near Naples, a gladiator named Spartacus escaped to lead a revolt of slaves in 73–71 BC. Gladiators lived in **barracks**, like soldiers, and the remains of the gladiator barracks at Pompeii can still be seen today.

A piece of glass painted with pictures of gladiators. The man on the right is a *retiarius*, with his trident. He is fighting an armoured swordsman. Found at Vindolanda in Britain, this glass was made in Germany and may have belonged to the commander of the Vindolanda **fort**.

Through these tunnels, gladiators and wild animals made their way into the Colosseum in Rome. Criminals and Christians also took their last journeys into the arena, to die for the crowd's amusement. During one series of 'games', it was common for hundreds of people and thousands of animals to be killed.

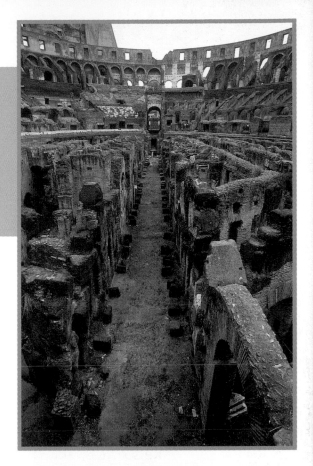

Fights to the death

In the arena, several pairs of gladiators often fought at the same time. A favourite pairing was a net-man, or *retiarius*, against a chaser, or *secutor*. The net-man wore little armour, and carried a net and a long three-pronged spear. His opponent wore armour, including a helmet, and fought with a sword. From records of betting on the fights, it seems that the quicker-moving net-man had slightly the better chance of winning. Pictures also show gladiators fighting wild animals, such as leopards and bears.

Fights were to the death, but the crowd could save the life of a wounded man who had fought well, by asking the watching emperor to spare him. If the emperor agreed, the wounded man was carried out of the arena. If the emperor disagreed, the winner had to kill his defeated opponent, whose body was then dragged away by attendants dressed as demons from the **Underworld**.

Women in the arena

There were almost certainly a few women gladiators. Female fighters are shown in statues and mentioned by writers. Museum of London experts have found the bones of a woman they believe was a gladiator in Roman London. One clue is a lamp buried with her, which has a picture of a fallen gladiator. Interestingly, her burial place was outside a known Roman cemetery. Gladiators were probably buried separately from other people.

41

Studying the Romans at work

We know about the Romans at work from what they left behind. They built everywhere they went. Few people in history left so much concrete evidence of their achievements.

Some Roman writers, such as Virgil and Columella, tell us in detail about the work that went on in the countryside. Other writers, like Vitruvius, wrote about Roman technology and machines. Ordinary people wrote too, and from sites like Pompeii we can read graffiti – writing scratched on walls, tiles or pots.

Pompeii: a site that tells a story

Many Roman towns have been excavated by **archaeologists**. None is more remarkable than Pompeii, a seaside town on the Bay of Naples in Italy.

The Roman writer Pliny the Younger tells how on 24 August AD 79, Pompeii was destroyed by an eruption of the volcano Vesuvius. Pompeii was buried by ash, almost 4 metres deep. It was never rebuilt, and lay hidden and forgotten. People first started to dig into the ruins in the 1700s, and by the late 1900s much of the town had been uncovered. Roofs fell in, crushed by the weight of ash, but walls and streets remained hardly damaged.

The Macellum was Pompeii's main food market. Here people came to buy fresh fruit, vegetables, meat and fish. A tank full of water was probably used to keep live fish in. Fish bones have been found in the market drains.

The larger of Pompeii's two theatres was open to the sky, and had room for 5000 people. In the town, visitors can see houses, gardens, paintings, even 'beware of the dog' signs.

Pompeii gives us a glimpse into the everyday lives of Roman workers. Food remains give clues as to what they cooked in their kitchens. From Pompeii, we know what kind of workshops and shops there were in the town, even how many bakers' shops the citizens could visit.

Workers of the empire

In this book, you have seen how Romans worked, and learned about some of the jobs they did. Mostly these jobs were done without the help of machines. Tasks such as weaving and metalworking involved skills learned slowly over generations. These job skills were passed on from parent to child, and from master to apprentice.

All these jobs had their place within the Roman economy for over 500 years. Skills used by Romans at work found their way all over the **empire**.

What archaeologists look for
By examining Pompeii and other Roman sites, archaeologists have discovered a lot about the jobs that were done there. In museums, we can see tools Roman workers used. We can see the things they made, such as coins, shoes, iron tools, glass and pottery. Occasionally buried treasure comes to light, such as jewellery or a silver dish, which shows how skilled Roman workers could be.

Timeline

Sources and further reading

Sources

Daily Life in Ancient Rome,
Florence Dupont (Blackwell, 1992)
The English Heritage Book of Villas and the Roman Countryside,
Guy de la Bedoyere (English Heritage/Batsford 1993)
The Great Invasion,
Leonard Cottrell (Evans Brothers, 1958)
Greece and Rome at War,
Peter Connolly (Macdonald, 1981)
Roman Britain,
Peter Salway (Oxford University Press, 1992)
Roman Britain,
H. H. Scullard (Thames and Hudson, 1994)
The Roman Invasion of Britain,
Graham Webster (Batsford, 1993)
Roman London,
Hall and Merrifield (HMSO/Museum of London, 1986)
Roman Towns in Britain,
Guy de la Bedoyere (English Heritage/Batsford 1992)
Women in Roman Britain,
Lindsay Allason-Jones (British Museum, 1989)

Further reading

Ancient Rome,
Mike Corbishley (Facts on File/Equinox, 1989)
Family Life in Roman Britain,
Peter Chrisp (Hodder Wayland, 2001)
Look Inside a Roman Villa,
Peter Chrisp (Hodder Wayland, 2002)
Roman Villas and Great Houses,
Brenda Williams (Heinemann, 1997)
What Happened Here?: Roman Palace,
Tim Wood (A & C Black, 2000)

Glossary

altar table or other special place for making religious offerings

amphitheatre large circular stadium, with an arena or sanded area

anatomy study of the human body

aqueducts pipe or bridge-like structure for carrying water into towns

archaeologist expert on the past who studies objects and evidence often uncovered from beneath the soil or under the sea

astrology belief that the stars and planets influence people's lives

auxiliary soldier who was not a Roman citizen

barracks building where soldiers live and sleep

basilica building used as a city hall and law courts

bellows bag like pump for blowing air into a fire to make it hotter

bribery payment in return for a favour, usually illegal

centurion officer roughly equivalent to a sergeant in a modern army, in charge of a century (between 80 and 100 men)

chaff dry outer part (husk) of an ear of wheat or other cereal plant

citizen Roman man entitled to vote in elections and serve in the legions

civil servant person working for the government, carrying out day-to-day business

comedies amusing or light-hearted plays

consul highest government official in the Roman republic; two consuls were elected each year

crop rotation planting different crops in a field, from one year to the next

dictated means 'read out'; when one person read out a letter for another person to write

emperor supreme ruler of Rome; the first ruler to hold the Latin title *imperator* was Augustus

empire large area with many peoples living under rule of an emperor

excavated means cleared or revealed by archaeologists digging into the ground

flail farm tool for threshing grain, often a heavy weight on the end of a cord or chain

fort building made to keep out enemies, with walls, ditches and towers

guild organization of workers in the same trade

historian someone who writes about past events and people

interest fee charged by a moneylender, perhaps 10 per cent of the loan

legate commander of a legion and governor of a province

legion main battle unit of the Roman army, numbering at various times between 4000 and 6000 legionaries

litter enclosed seat or couch for riding in, carried by slaves

magistrate someone who acts as a judge in a law court

manure animal dung used to enrich soil for growing crops

mine place from which rocks containing metals such as silver or iron, or minerals such as salt are dug out of the ground

mosaic decoration used on wall and floors, using small stones to make pictures and patterns

myth story about gods and legendary deeds

omens signs sent by the gods

overseer foreman, a man in charge of other workers

oxen cattle used to pull ploughs and carts

papyrus kind of paper made in Egypt, from reed plants

parchment thin writing material made from the skins of animals

provinces territories conquered and ruled by Romans, such as Britannia (Britain) and Gaul

quarries holes in ground where sand and stone are cut, for building use

quay place where a ship unloads its cargo

republic form of government in early Rome, with elected officials, not a king

sacrifice offering made to the gods, often of an animal newly killed

scythe long-handled tool for cutting wheat and grass

Senate Rome's parliament, made up of important people and former officials, who advised the elected consuls

sickle curved knife for cutting wheat and grass

sirens supernatural witch-like beings whose songs were supposed to lure seamen to disaster

spinning twisting fibres together to make thread

surveyor person who planned routes of Roman roads

tragedies serious plays often with an unhappy ending

Underworld dark and gloomy place to which Romans believed people went after death

urine liquid waste from the body, got rid of when we go to the toilet

will instructions about what a person wants done after his or her death

Index